OP-TRICKS

CREATING KINETIC ART

BY MICKEY KLAR MARKS

KINETICS BY EDITH ALBERTS

PHOTOGRAPHED BY DAVID ROSENFELD

J. B. LIPPINCOTT COMPANY • PHILADELPHIA • NEW YORK

FOR NAT, ISIE, ROBERT, AND ANDREW

U.S. Library of Congress Cataloging in Publication Data

Marks, Mickey Klar.
  Op-tricks: creating kinetic art.

  SUMMARY: Step-by-step instructions, accompanied by photographs, for creating art that "tricks" the eye and gives the illusion of movement in painting.
  1. Kinetic art—Juvenile literature. [1. Kinetic art. 2. Art—Technique] I. Alberts, Edith, illus. II. Rosenfeld, David, birth date, illus. III. Title.
N6494.K5M37   702'.8   79-38550
ISBN-0-397-31217-2 (lib. bdg.)   ISBN-0-397-31291-1 (pbk.)

OP-TRICKS CREATING KINETIC ART

Speed is this century's second name. Our spinning world seems to go faster and faster. Scientific discoveries are practically weekly events, and art is not at the tail end of this progress but part of it.

In kinetic art, the artist has tried to capture motion, to hold on to a fleeting image, to find an artistic expression that exists this second, right now!

The word *kinetic,* from Greek *kinetikos,* means "pertaining to motion." Thus, this art form is generally known as kinetic art, sometimes called "op" (for optical) art. The interplay of shapes, the placement of lines, the vibrations of color upon color, reflected light, all create changing optical effects. The works themselves may be static, but the eye becomes a camera when looking at a kinetic; there is an instantaneous reflex that triggers the shutter and forces the eye itself to move.

This mind-bursting art form is limitless, encompassing the use not only of light and space and motion but also of constructions, sculptured forms, painting, and electrical and mechanical devices. In this book we will concentrate on painting, simple construction, and some examples of object media.

With a few basic materials, we want to start you moving toward creating moving art.

You will undoubtedly find some of the things you will need right in your own house, such as a ruler, a compass, glue-all, a pencil, and nails. All other materials that are needed will be listed before each project.

You know you can't bake a cake without the right ingredients and the simplest way to get a good result is to have those ingredients on the kitchen table. So make life easy for yourself and have all your materials at hand and an idea for a composition in your head before you pick up your pencil to start.

In every art book we have ever done we have parroted the same advice over and over again. This book is not meant to be anything other than a guide to techniques and materials. It is not meant to teach you to make carbon copies of the examples depicted here. It is only to spark your interest and imagination, to give you the mechanics that you may not be familiar with so that you can "do your own thing."

*M*OTO PERPETUA

MATERIALS
Plywood or extra-thick cardboard, white spray paint, plastic sticking tapes in various widths and colors, ruler, and pencil.

1. Spray plywood board. Let dry.

2. Lay the board in a horizontal position and draw pencilled lines about 2 inches from the top of the board and 2 inches from the bottom of the board.

3. Starting at the top, place the first strip of tape on the edge of the line. Run the tape across the board leaving an inch of extra tape on each end. Press the loose ends of the tape over the edges of the board.

4. Using the second color, apply the next strip of tape leaving a hairline of space between the stripes.

5. Continue adding strips of various widths and colors, stopping on the pencilled guide line.

Is this painting moving? Yes? No?

Hang it up and walk around the room looking at it from different angles. It holds a surprise because the various widths, different colors, and placement of the tapes creates a waving, slightly dizzying effect.

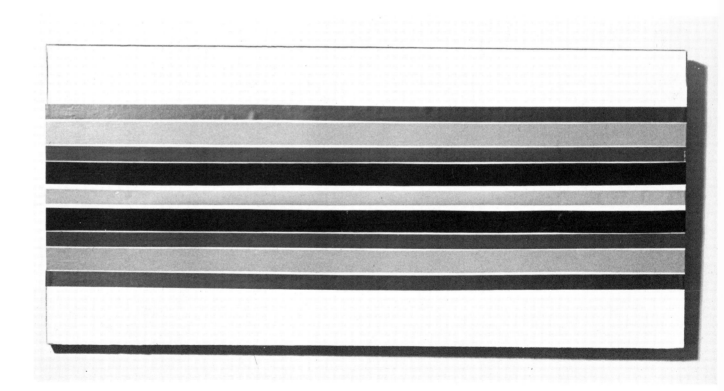

BRAILLE

MATERIALS

Pencil, ruler, compass, white all-purpose sketch paper, a turkish towel, bath mat, or any firm, soft surface, and a nail.

You can use any size paper that you wish. This particular sheet was taken from a standard 17 × 14 sketch pad.

1. With the pencil and ruler draw a border approximately 2 inches from the edge of the paper.

2. Leaving an inch of space, draw a second border inside the first rectangle.

3. Draw a third border, again leaving an inch of space.

4. Starting from the third border (or inside line), find the center of the rectangle by drawing a diagonal line from the upper left-hand corner to the lower right-hand corner and a line from the upper right-hand corner to the lower left-hand corner with pencil and ruler.

The center point is where the two lines cross.

5. Make a circle within the rectangular frames with the compass, using the cross as your center point. Erase guide lines.

6. Draw a second circle inside the first circle leaving about an inch of space.

7. In the dead center of the pencilled circles draw a small circle about the size of a silver dollar.

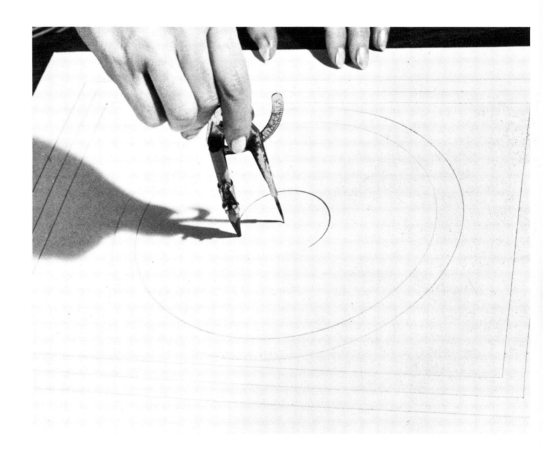

8. Lay the paper on a towel or any other soft surface and punch holes using a large nail following the outlined design. Punch holes approximately every ¼ inch. Punch holes on all pencilled lines.

9. Punch holes at random in the center circle.

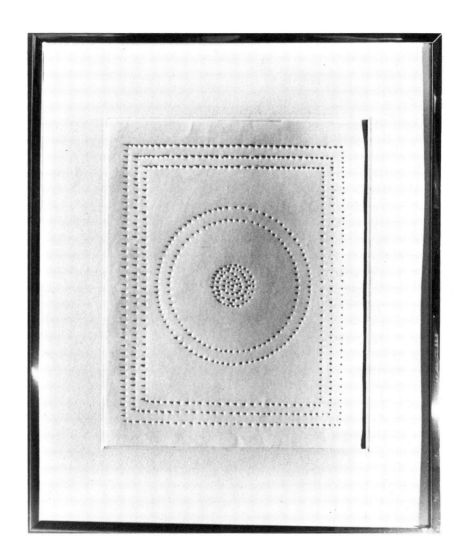

10.   Turn the paper over. The raised side is your finished work. Mat and frame.

The strength of this painting depends on the position or brightness of your source of light. The dots protrude and form shadows against the white background. It is important to hang this work so that the dots cast playful shadows.

Straight Line Drawings

It is exciting to discover how many illusions can be created by drawing straight lines. The eye sees circles, curves, loops, and arcs but is constantly and mischievously fooled.

The next group of paintings is designed to play those tricks, yet every line will be as straight as a fence post.

Before you start any of the following projects, take some scrap paper and draw a series of lines, using a ruler and a felt-tip marking pen. Wipe the ruler after every line on a piece of rag, paper towel, or cleansing tissue.

In all of the straight line kinetics precision and neatness are essential. In case of an error, such as a small smudge or a slip of a line, take white poster paint and paint over the mistake. Nothing will cover too many smudges or too many squiggles.

In most of the following drawings a ½-inch scale is used for demonstration purposes, but in original work of your own any scale of equal measurements can be used.

When you buy your ink markers, whether black or color, be sure they are permanent. There are water-soluble markers but you won't be needing them for any of the work in this book since we hope your artistic endeavors will be good enough to last a long time.

The same materials will be used for all straight line paintings. They are: a ruler, compass, pencil, art gum eraser, rag or paper towel, thin and thick felt-tip marking pens, and 14 × 14 all-purpose sketch paper. Heavy quality paper is preferable.

INTEGRA 1

1. Divide the paper into four equal parts using the pencil and ruler. The squares will measure 7 inches each.

2. Find the center of each square by drawing a diagonal line from its upper left-hand corner and from its upper right-hand corner to its lower left-hand corner with pencil and ruler.

   Mark a small cross at the center point.

3. Using the center point of each square draw a circle approximately 4 inches in diameter with the compass.

4.   Mark dots with pencil and ruler every ¼-inch on all outside edges of the square.

5.   Starting with the upper left-hand square, using the dots as a guide, draw straight lines within the pencilled circle from top to bottom with the thick ink marker.

6. In the square directly below, again using the dots as your guide, draw straight lines within the circle going from left to right.

7. Duplicate the lines of the upper left circle in the lower right circle.

8. Draw lines in the lower left circle to match the circle on the upper right.

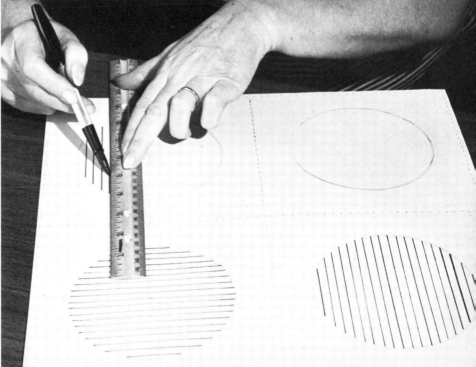

9. Starting again in the top left-hand square and using the ruler and thin ink marker, draw straight lines within the square connecting the ¼-inch dots from left to right, being sure you do not draw any lines into the circle.

Always work away from the last line you drew so that your work is visible to you and to prevent smudging.

10. Repeat Step 9 in lower right square.

11. In the upper right and lower left squares, draw lines with the ink marker from top to bottom.

12. Erase all pencil marks.

If you hadn't worked on this project yourself, would you believe this composition was made up of straight lines?

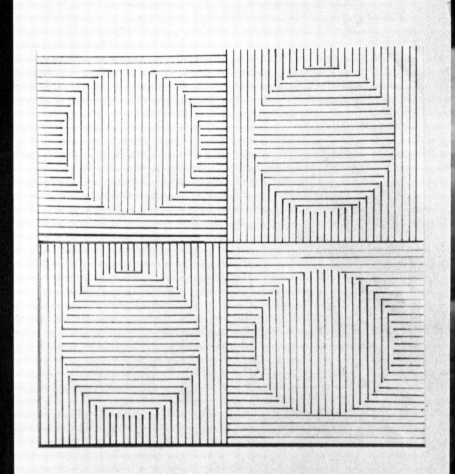

INTEGRA 2

The following painting, which gives a totally different effect, is actually a blowup or enlargement, if you will, of one of the squares in the previous project, with a slight addition. The difference is a matter of dimension.

1. Mark dots every ½-inch on all outside edges of the paper with pencil and ruler.

2. Find the center of the paper as you did in Integra I.

3. Mark a large circle with the compass.

4. With a thick ink marker, in any color other than black, connect the ½-inch dots to form the circle, working from top to bottom and staying within the pencilled circle as before.

5. Using the ½-inch dots as the guide, draw vertical lines with the wide ink marker, being certain not to enter the pencilled circle.

6. Starting at the right-hand horizontal line at the top of the circle, draw a 2-inch line with the fine black ink marker. Continue until you get to the bottom of the circle.

7. Add vertical lines along the left-hand side of the vertical lines within the circle as shown in the final photograph.

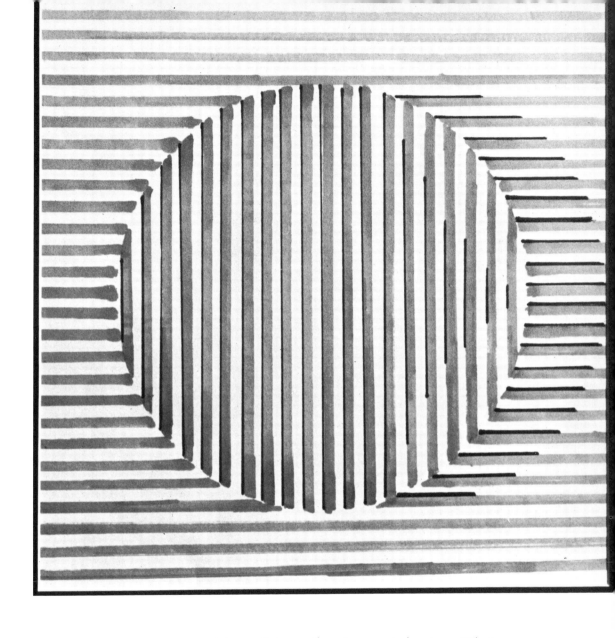

8.   Erase all pencilled lines.

Integra 2 is another innocent deceiver. What appears to be a spinning ball was actually drawn without one curved line.

INTEGRA 3

1. Draw a free form creating any shape you like. We have used four straight lines of unequal length.

2. Make a circle inside the free form with the compass.

3. Starting at any point of the outer edge of the circle, draw multiple lines with ruler and marking pen.

4. Keep moving the ruler in the same direction, always coming in contact with a small portion of the pencilled circle and ending at the outer edge of the free form.

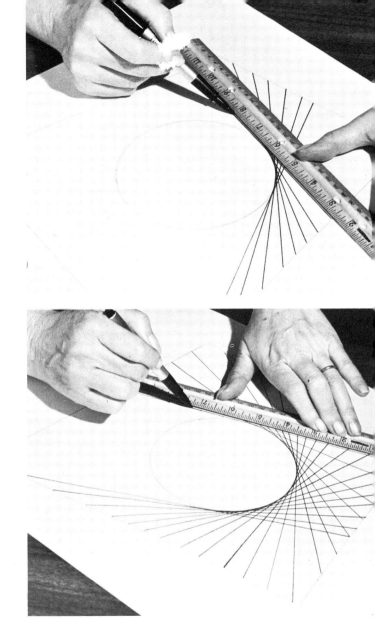

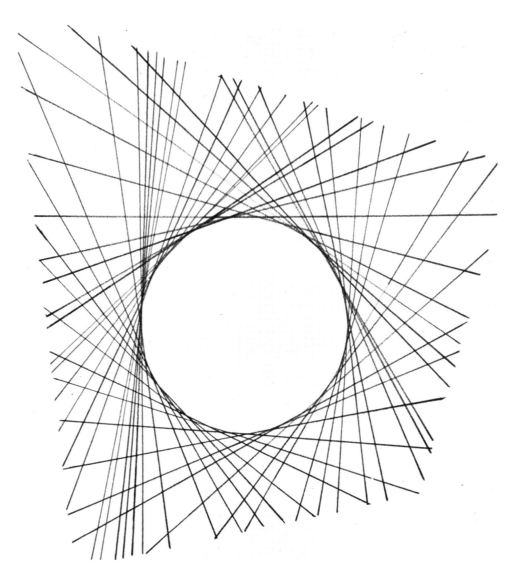

5. Continue drawing straight lines with the marking pen around the circle until every bit of the pencilled circle is no longer visible.

6. Erase the four outside lines of the free form. Magically the straight lines you have drawn become a perfect sphere.

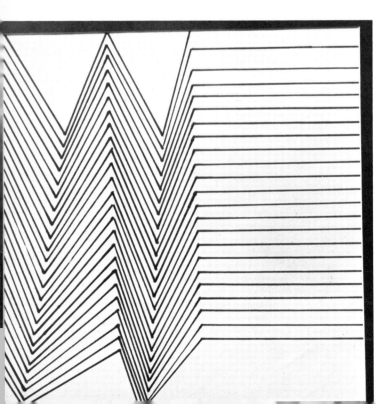

Here are three more straight line drawings for you to experiment with.

INTEGRA 4

This drawing starts with random slanted lines. Dots are placed every ½ inch along the slanted lines and the edges of the paper.

The dots are guides in forming the zigzag pattern as well as insuring that the mulitple lines are equidistant.

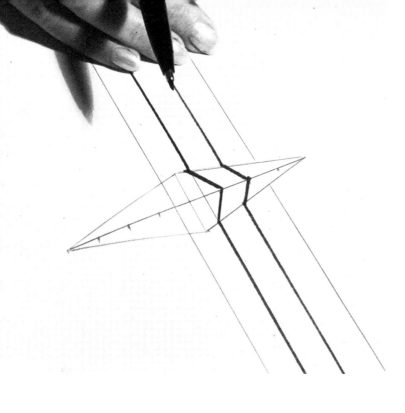

INTEGRA 5

In this drawing ½-inch dots on left and right of the sketch paper become the guide for the horizontal lines that stop outside of the diamond shape. The lines angle inside the diamond pattern as shown in the photograph.

Several diamond patterns of different sizes may be used. Only three were drawn here to create a balanced composition. Remember to erase all visible pencil marks.

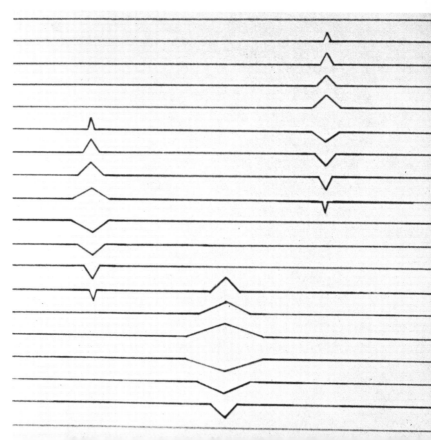

INTEGRA 6

Now that you know all the tricks of straight line drawings here's a teaser that you can puzzle out all by yourself.

REFLECTIONS 1

MATERIALS
Pencil, paper, plexiglass, wide felt-tip ink markers (any colors you wish), monofilament fishing line or very thin cord or picture wire.

Plexiglass can be bought in sheets at lumberyards or hardware stores. The lumberyard will cut the plexiglass to size and also drill the holes you will need in order to hang the work. We suggest using monofilament fishing line rather than cord or wire for hanging Reflections, since, for the best effect, the painting should look as if it is hanging in space.

1. Draw a design on sketch paper the exact size of the piece of plexiglass.

2. Place the plexiglass over the sketch.

3. With the ink marker, trace and fill in your composition.

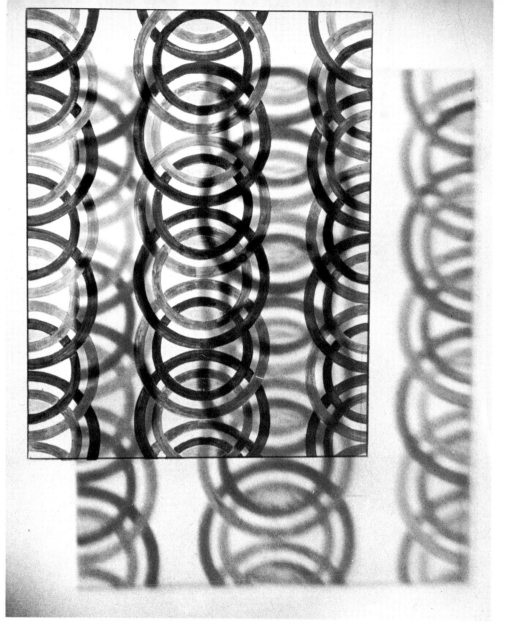

4. Finish coloring the plexiglass, then thread the fishing line through the holes and hang the painting from the ceiling far enough from a wall so that the light is able to come through.

Remember that the above project is only an example, but when you do an original be sure to leave large areas unpainted, for the enchantment of this kinetic depends on reflected light.

REFLECTIONS 2

A simple yet dramatically effective piece can be made by using the same materials as in the preceding project, then mounted on a stand for display.

In Reflections 1 and 2 the interplay of color and light tantalizes the viewer. Look at the works in daylight, then in artificial light. The patterns shift from hour to hour and offer variations that are constantly exciting.

SUPER BLOCKS

MATERIALS
Plexiglass, plastic cement, or an adhesive that dries clear, plastic boxes of any size or shape—such as ring boxes, pill boxes, pin boxes, clip boxes, etc. You probably have boxes of this kind in your own house. If not, you can purchase empty ones in various shapes and colors at any dime, gift, or drug store.

1. Structure the boxes in an arrangement that pleases your eye, such as the tiered geometric kinetic photographed below.

2. Glue the boxes into place. Let dry for about half an hour. Mount on a stand.

By filling a few of the boxes with sand, salt, or crushed colored chalk, or partially filling one or two of the plastic containers with spices, such as paprika or dry mustard, grains of sugar, or a few tea leaves, you can create variations that change the entire composition and give it a new dimension.

Would you like to turn this kinetic into a construction without using any mechanical device?

Buy one or two Mexican jumping beans (novelty and toy stores carry them). Put them in the plastic boxes. The beans' mysterious but natural engine will literally move in the Super Blocks.

OPTIMA

MATERIALS
Wall cork, plywood, glue-all, push pins.

Wall cork can be bought at any lumberyard and can be cut with a knife. A piece of plywood for backing is advisable, since cork tends to shred if worked too much. You can have the wood as well as the cork cut to size at the lumberyard if you prefer.

Push pins (you will need at least one hundred for this kinetic) can be found in dime stores, hardware stores, stationery stores, etc. In the following project we have used plastic and aluminum pins for variable effect.

1. Glue cork to the plywood backing.

2. Make a sketch or several sketches on scrap paper until you come up with a composition you like.

3. Following your working drawing, press the
    push pins into the cork.

Working on cork is fun. Instead of doing preliminary sketches you might want to play around and create a design as you go along. You can rearrange the push pins as often as you like. The effects you can achieve are limitless and you can have a new artwork to show any time you feel you want a change of scene. Once again light is the source that vibrates this work. The different textures of the aluminum and plastic push pins seem to drift and sway in various directions, depending not only on the light but on the angle from which it is viewed.

SEE SAW

MATERIALS

Plywood, white spray paint, monofilament fishing line, five nails (two inches in length) scissors, darning needle, compass, silver adhesive-backed paper.

Silver adhesive-backed paper comes by the yard and can be bought at art stores, hardware stores, or wallpaper or do-it-yourself furniture shops.

1. Spray board. Let dry.

2. Draw 60 2-inch circles with the compass on the back of the silver paper.

3. Cut out the 60 discs with a small scissors.

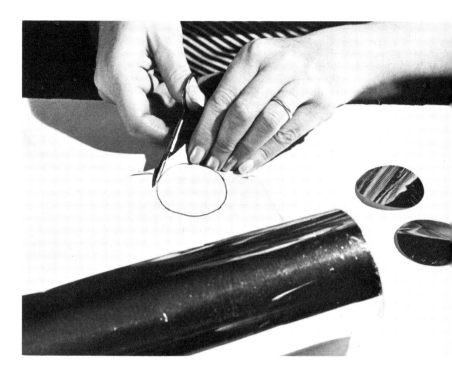

4. Remove backing from one disc and join it back-to-back with the second disc. Repeat with the remainder of the discs. You will then have 30 circular silver pieces.

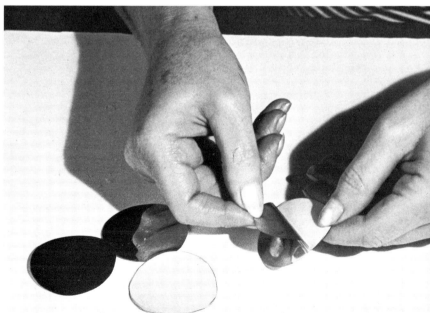

5.   Place 5 discs at equal distances apart along the top of the board. Hammer a nail through the center of each disc.

6.   Lift the disc to the head of the nail.

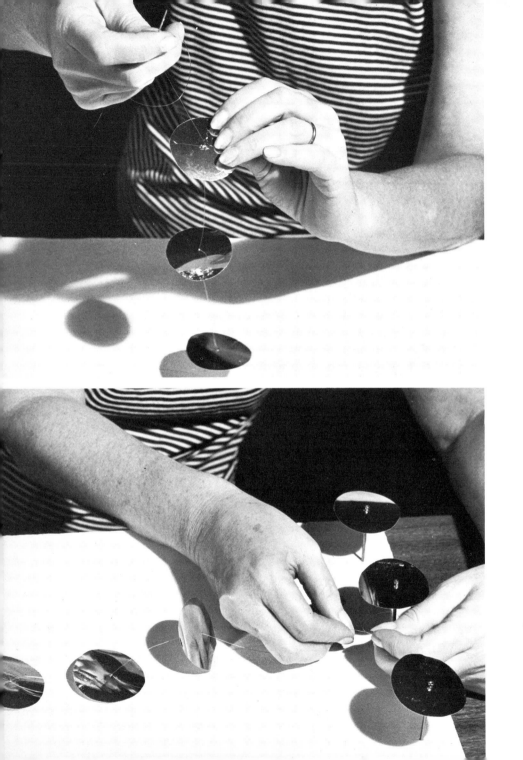

7. Cut a length of monofilament line a couple of inches longer than the board. Thread the needle. Make a knot at the bottom of the line.

8. Stick the needle into the center of one of the remaining discs. Slide the disc down to the knot. Leave approximately 3 inches of line and make another knot.

9. Repeat the same process, stopping the disc at the second knot. Repeat until you have 5 silver discs on the length of line.

10. Tie the line to one of the nails at the top of the board.

11.   Repeat steps 9 and 10 until all discs have been sewn and tied.

Any air current stirs this kinetic into motion and rotates the discs, creating prisms that not only bounce off the board but dance around the room.

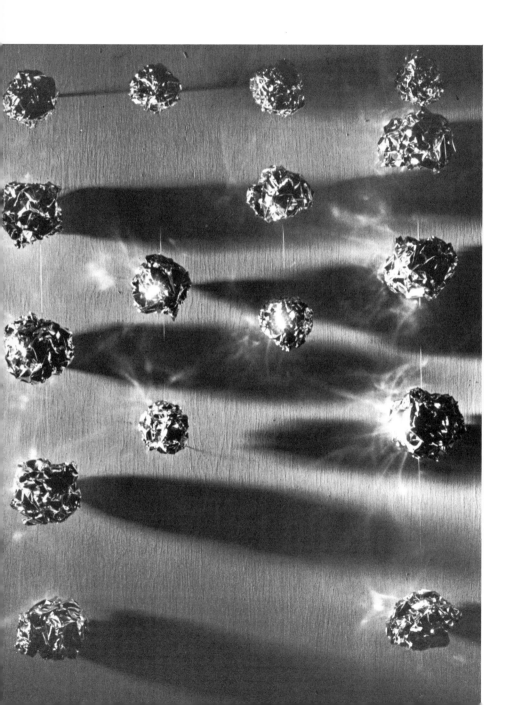

WAVE LENGTHS

A similar reflective kinetic using the same materials as were used in See Saw and following the same instructions can be created, with one change. Instead of using silver adhesive-backed paper use heavy-duty tinfoil (the kind that comes in rolls and can be found in any grocery or supermarket).

Cut out 16 10-inch squares of foil and form into balls.

INNER DIMENSIONS

MATERIALS
Drawing paper, wide magic marker, ruler, pencil, compass, and scissors.

1. Draw horizontal stripes with the ink marker all the way across the paper (the width of the ruler).

2. Turn the paper over. Draw vertical straight lines 2 inches apart with pencil and ruler.

3. With the compass, draw circles at random within the vertical pencil lines.

4. Cut out the circles with a small scissors.

5. Fold the paper on vertical pencil lines to make accordion pleats.

6. The finished kinetic can be placed on a table, desk, or bookshelf.

If you would prefer to use Inner Dimensions on a wall rather than free standing, cut a piece of silver adhesive-backed paper the same size as a piece of plywood. Press the adhesive side of the paper to the board. Glue the side edges of the kinetic and gently press to the mirrored reflector board.

Why does this kinetic seem to be moving? The folds turn the straight lines into wavy ones. The holes vary in depth when seen from different angles and go into semieclipse like little moons.

Mickey Klar Marks was born in Brooklyn and moved to Manhattan when she was a child. She remained in the city, studying drama, poetry, and the other fine arts, until she and her husband moved to Armonk, New York, where she happily indulges herself in sports and hobbies. Other books by Mickey Klar Marks are *Painting Free* and *Collage*.

Edith Alberts, who created the kinetics for this book, is a retired fashion model, an interior designer, a sculptor, and a painter. Born in Haverhill, Massachusetts, she now lives in Waban, Massachusetts. Her previous books are *Collage* and *Painting Free*, which were also done in collaboration with Mickey Klar Marks.